not my daughter

not my daughter
poems

Jessie Scrimager Galloway

Etched Press
San Francisco

Copyright © 2024 Jessie Scrimager Galloway
All rights reserved.

ISBN 978-1-935847-12-0

Library of Congress Cataloging-in-Publication Data on file
Library of Congress Control Number: 2024930080

No part of this publication may be reproduced, or stored in a retrieval system, or transmitted in any form or by any means, electronic, mechanical, photocopying, recording, or otherwise without written permission except for use in creative or critical reviews for the purposes of education.

Cover design: Jessie Scrimager Galloway
Author photo: Reina Vazquez
Layout: Kevin Dublin

Purchase copies of this book by asking at your local bookstore or ordering online:

Etched Press
www.etchedpress.com

Also available on Amazon Kindle

Praise for *not my daughter*

"With crisp lyricism and narration, *not my daughter* slices dogma and illuminates the power of resiliency. This book is a must-have for living in this world and claiming your sexuality, your name, your life no matter what. Jessie's poems redefine daughterhood and embrace what we humans long for, always, love."

–Thea Matthews, author of *Unearth [The Flowers]*

"Jessie writes some of the most beautiful and affecting poetry I've ever read. This collection is a masterwork from beginning to end. This heart-wrenching collection shows how the most treacherous home lives can be hidden behind the neatest doors. Read these poems if you've ever felt the dissonance between the life you were given and the one you're desperately reaching for."

–Andrea Passwater, Oakland-based writer

"This debut collection presents a brilliant examination of three languages: heritage, erasure, and wonder. Here, you'll see a poet in the crossfire of the human experience. This work cuts with precision crafting a map that resonates with raw authenticity. She weaves a narrative that is both haunting and deeply moving. This book is a must-read."

–Anthony Fangary, author of *Haram*

"The queer adopted kid in me scrambles to find the queer adopted kid book club I can bring this collection to. The poet who teaches creative writing in me swoons over the brilliant craft, the unexpected and perfect play with language and design that points to masterful skill, and wants to use every poem as an example of "this is how you truth." The humanest human in me, who is queer and adopted and a poet, feels my human resonate with every word.

Jessie Galloway shares deeply personal and vulnerable lifestuff in poems that transcend the idiosyncratic and connect with the human in us all, most especially, I suspect, with those of us who have felt the deep loss of severed connections. This is a collection I'll visit again and again. And on days when I feel like I'm no one to anyone, that I don't proper-fit anywhere, I'll visit it yet again because there are many places to belong on these pages, poems that fit, poems that assure me I'm not alone."

–Su Flatt, Columbus-based writer & educator

Character Map

Mom=Julie, Birthmom, Natural Mother
Mother=Bess(ie), Adopted Mom
Dad=Phil, Adopted Dad
Grandpa & Grandma=parents of Bess, Mother, adopted mom

Also by Jessie Scrimager Galloway

Liminal: A Life of Cleavage (Lost Horse Press)
                                                  [as Lisa Galloway]

TABLE OF CONTENTS

Closed Adoption	1
Biographical Information Sheet	2
Hello, My Name Would've Been/Has Been/Is	3
You Ask, What Binds Me?	4
Multiple Choice	5
No One's Baby Shower	6
Origin Wound	7
Natural mother was interested in arts and crafts	8
To Know What You're Worth	9
White	10
Dear Dad,	11
Entry Way	12
Bessie	14
Heirlooms	15
Ode to My Texture Fetish, *origin unknown*	18
Sweet'n Low	19
Porcelain	21
Everyone Has a Tale	22
Naming	23
Have Mercy	24
In the Shadows	26
Disrupting the Literary Narrative	28
How Am I?	30
Envoy	31
Desperation	32

Mercy	33
The Language Of Arms	35
Grenade	36
I Drink	38
Too Late	39
Epitaph	41
Dust	44
Fists Are the Size of Hearts	45
Bessie	47
Catharsis	48
Fishing	50
The Logic of Dreams—Freudian, Predictable	51
Comfort	52
Smile For Me, Honey	53
So Many Deaths This Year	55
Homosexuals More Likely to Develop Bipolar Disorder	56
Shaping Desire	59
Barometer	60
Some Dance to Remember, Some Dance to Forget	61
Naming	62
Reflection at 45	64
acknowledgements	67
education guide	69
discussion guide	71
writing prompt	72
video poem	73
music playlist	75

Closed Adoption

My real mom is a fragmented paragraph
on a quarter-page
biographical information sheet
from a pink adoption folder
pinned on the bulletin board above my bed

with push pins, marked threads,
I hung myself
between sparse words
for forty years,
desperate for lineage,
I marked similarities,
believed with unwavering hope
that blood would see me whole.

My biology, the hole holding
it too big to stay the pin,
paper corner slit, my story
lopsided like a lobe giving
to a heavy earring.

Family Background Information

Your daughter was born on April 24, 1978, at 3:15 P.M. She weighed 5 lb. 13½ oz. and was 20" long.

The natural mother was 19 years old and described as being 5'4" tall, weighing 115 lbs. with red hair, blue eyes and a fair complexion. She was very healthy and received good prenatal care. She was a high school graduate and had been trained in respiratory therapy. She was an A and B student in school. She enjoyed arts and crafts. She had a pleasant personality.

The maternal grandfather was 43 years old and described as being 5'8" tall, weighing 160 lbs. with black hair, blue eyes and a dark complexion. He was a high school graduate and had received training on his job. The maternal grandmother was 43 years old and described as being 5' tall, weighing 100 lbs., with red hair, blue eyes, and a fair complexion. She was a high school graduate and had vocational training. The maternal great grandfather died at 64 from arterial sclerosis.

The natural mother had 3 siblings. Two had brown hair and one was reddish blonde. They all had blue eyes. They were all in good health and active in sports.

The natural father was 25 years old and described as being 5'8" tall, weighing 140 lbs. with light brown hair, blue eyes and a medium complexion. He had completed the 10th grade and was a B - C student. He worked in construction and was active in sports.

Hello, My Name Would've Been/Has Been/Is

Birth: _____ Scrimager
Foster family: Betsy Ann _____
Adopted if boy: Luke Michael Galloway
Adopted 1st choice if girl: Lindsay Marie Galloway
Adopted 2nd choice: Lisa Renee Galloway
My name is: Jessie Scrimager Galloway

You Ask, What Binds Me?

I am a spinning compass
a centrifuge of blood
no one
claims the origin

of my red woven
by incantations
from mom's mouth
which never kissed my cheek
I am someone's kid
knuckles tight   wielding
a flashlight to search the closet
for a way home at five.

I am the mother
of night terrors
monsters in mirrors
I conjured the ghosts
I am ether
to drown my mind
racing   toward
the always-more questions

I am looking both ways
to separate
the veil
of knowing
from all
I've had to unknow.

Multiple Choice

When you hear the word adoption, you think:

- ☐ Legally taking a child to bring up as your own

- ☐ Choosing to take up or use something

- ☐ Better off, lucky

- ☐ Little Orphan Annie

- ☐ All of the Above

- ☐ Other?

_____

No One's Baby Shower

Birthmom says she wanted me,
planned to keep me
'til eight months,
but birthdad moved
from pills to needles
to lost.

No one said, *congratulations*!
No one filled pastel balloons with helium,
hung twisted streamers, smoothed the
mint green tablecloth.

No one cut vegetables, made tiny cucumber
sandwiches with the crusts trimmed,
mixed the packet of Hidden Valley
for dip, and arranged the crudité platter.

No one made the heavily frosted cake,
no one joked, *c'mon, the baby's fully baked*,
as they suggested adding vodka
to orange sherbert, 7-up, cranberry juice punch.

No one rolled their eyes
at the diaper games.
No one spouted ungrateful complaints
that the family is cheap, because the gifts
were mostly onesies and pacifiers.
No one placed their hand on mom's belly,
felt me kick, tried to predict my gender.

Origin Wound

Snip.

We became paper.

    Pressed type.

Erasure.

        Xeroxes.

Natural mother and

    [name],

white, baby girl.

Natural mother was interested in arts and crafts

Her prayers laced through veins,
fingers pressed in steeples,
wrists resting atop her belly,
crossing anima, animus, X and Y,

I was stitched by her whispers—
bits of tissue anchored two
psyches, she carved
the base of my spine—

its grounded wings,
she stacked tiny bone fists
each a wish, instruction, moored by
her marrow—central, nervous hope.

She painted our stories
inside my skull—her cathedral ceilings.

She separated the sea in stained glass,
chipped sky to match our eyes.

To Know What You're Worth

SUEMMA COLEMAN AGENCY
512 East Minnesota St.
Indianapolis, Indiana 46203

ADOPTIVE HOME PLACEMENT AGREEMENT

This agreement made and entered into this 1st day of May, 1978, between Suemma Coleman Agency, hereinafter designated as "Agency", and Phillip & Bessie Galloway, hereinafter designated as "Foster Parents", with reference to the placement and possible adoption of Betsy Ann / April 24, 1978.
Name of Child / Date of Birth

Said Agency has this day delivered, and said Foster Parents have accepted, custody of the above named child with a view to adoption of said child by said Foster Parents six (6) months from this date.

It is understood and agreed that adoption is the legal act whereby an adult person takes another person into the relationship of parent and child and thereby secures the rights and incurs the responsibilities of a parent in respect to the person so adopted.

It is understood and agreed that said Foster Parents may, at any time within six (6) months from date hereof, and before said child is legally adopted, return said child to the Agency if the child is found unsatisfactory, or if for any reason the said Foster Parents decide they should not keep her. It is further agreed that the Agency reserves the right to remove the child from said Foster Parents at any time previous to legal adoption if at any time in the judgment of the Agency such removal is for the best interests of the child, and we, as prospective Foster Parents, waive any and all rights to question or dispute the judgment of said Agency in its removal of said child.

It is understood and agreed that the Foster Parents shall not, under any circumstances, give the child into the custody of any other person or institution without the consent of the Agency.

Said Foster Parents agree to provide said child with all food, clothing, shelter, medical attention and other necessities at their own cost and expense; and also agree that until the final adoption, by proper legal proceedings, the said child is in their care subject to supervision of said Agency.

It is further understood and agreed between said Agency and said Foster Parents that the Foster Parents named herein are paying the sum of $ 4,492.95 for its expense, including social and medical, which sum shall be in full settlement of all charges against said Foster Parents.

Signed on behalf of the Agency:

Foster Parents:
Bessie A. Galloway

White

Like mother's angels, her Jesus, and
the only-for-holidays tablecloth,
like bacon grease spooned into cast iron,
chopped potatoes soaking,
ice cube trays twisted to pop,
Corel plates thrown and proven to break.
Like *pass me the salt.*
Pour me a glass of milk.

Like, the taste of Dove soap,
the vanilla of Yankee candles.
Like mother's frayed nightgown—
moonlight, bone, the nativity.
Like Styrofoam, powdered creamer,
& grandpa's Basic Light.

Dear Dad,

I know you wanted a boy. Wanted to name him Luke. Dreamed he'd live out your sports scholarship dreams that were squashed by a busted knee and Vietnam drafting. But, *white baby girl* came up on the list, so you taught me to throw.

Bird claw my hand, line up stitching, count during windmill windup: 1, 2, 3, audibly add *umph* on *four*, flick and release my wrist, and follow through.

Make the first one fast, try for the inside, just inside their kneecaps. Scare 'em a little. Intimidation is your friend. Only hit them if they're a known slugger and they've got men on base. Then, cross-lace and aim straight across the plate. Give 'em something to swing at. Trust your team in the field. Now, practice. The game depends on you.

Entry Way

I was five when we moved in.
Dad was all blowtorch
and putty knife.
One plank at a time,
careful to pick around the nails.
This unpainting,
this stripping
was serious business.
The staircase,
the mantel,
all of the pieces
holding together the entryway.

Mother with that chandelier.
Goddamn, the gurgly brown water
in the sink while she washed the crystal
that would clink together later
when I stomped the stairs or
Dad slammed the door.

You know, the way
the sound of glass
pinging came to represent
our differences.

Remember how the front door peephole
rainbow-lit the foyer, the hallway—
to the kitchen wall— all the way a mix
of dust— light whirling.

I used to dance
in the crossfire
hoping to combust.

Bessie

Everyone drove to Williamsburg, KY.
Routes through the hills like her varicose veins
branching the states. Eight kids and all their's
holed up at Budget Inn on Highway 25.
Great-grandma Bessie, my adopted mother's
namesake, finally deteriorated
beyond her years-gone mind.

Grandpa brought his fishing chair down,
emptied a can of Coke for butts,
readied himself to sit and smoke.
He bought a flyswatter
from the hotel desk,
set about a single-handed mission to
keep us kids in line while ridding
his hometown of more vermin.

The early afternoon burial,
I stayed back, played Marco Polo, waved sparklers,
spelled out my name
amongst the chittering grandchildren.
A picture taken of me with Matt,
their only red-head, same age,
proof to assuage all the kin I belonged,
proof to me I could have
been born in-to this.

Heirlooms

Mother,
I prayed,
played in
rough lace,
covert abrasions,
tomboy trees
climbing, straddling limbs,
the rugged pink, the breaking
perversity of lust,
I am your
daughter.
Holding breath
for baptism,
holding the familiar
weight of bosoms,
like apples,
I salt the sweet bite of fruit,
Mother.

Bells ringing from all the churches
mornings of my childhood,
silty basements, I kept my eyes
on tan tiles, lace bobby socks, patent leather heels.
Dragged mine to mark across cracks,
lines and lines—
impatient matching disciples to
deeds, I preferred
Sunday school games like

Mother, may I
take one step forward?

*Lisa Renee, git over here right now.
We don't do that in this family.*

There is pleasure left in lunar imprints, the linger of
bruises on a bicep.

These Baptists shake trees
blocks at a time, bend limbs to snap,
it is me—remember, I am your
daughter.

Switches lashed against me
bent over a banquet table.

Go wash your hands.

Christmas was rapt by
the rattle of plates, the salt
of streaming tears.
Thank you Lord [and Leviticus] *for blessing us with
this meal.*

Pass the salt.
Take obscene bites.
Ask for another piece of ham.
    Take, eat:

this is my body,
broken for you.

Great-grandmother's china,
pattern worn
by fork scraping, scouring.
I would not
have chosen this red.
I would not
have taken their name
except in vain.
I would not have begged, *please don't*,
she would not have spit

you are
not my
                daughter
you are
not my

But, I am,
even without you,

still searching for
sated communion—
the milk-drunk gurgle of
a breastfed mouth.

Ode to My Texture Fetish, *origin unknown*

You ask me what brings me ecstatic joy,
sharing that you think of thongs,
even neon, even the repetitive Sisquo song,

but better and before, I think of
the texture trove of her black lace bodysuit,
crotch removed,

I will always choose
the pleasure of patterns,
the snap of, the finger-
sized holes
in fishnet tights
tangled in my grip
readying a well timed rip.

When not in haste, I relish the tease
abrading my face—
a cheek-rub friction
is rapture,
but I get caught
by the staccato of her
breath, and
I want—
and I want—
right now
to taste the catch
in the wetness of her moan.
Yes. Yes.

Sweet'n Low

Cracker Barrel, Gas City, IN 2003

I met Mother halfway between
our cities, waiting with a pink gift bag,
a wooden angel holding a butterfly—
a gift for Mother's Day. We sat awkward.
Disagreed on what movie I saw first,
she swore Cinderella,

I took you, we sat in front.

Two pink packets, sides torn, tossed,
granulated saccharin—

No, it was Bambi. I went with Dad, downtown, I was 5.
Remember, he gave me my nickname in softball—
    Thumper.
I stepped on a baby rabbit warming up to pitch.

a white rapid into
the translucent brown,   I'm thinking of baby
    deer,

I was lost with you.

the ice tea spoon swirl, clink, swirl, clink,

Cousin Vickie reads and writes,

faster—swink swink swink,

she would have been a better mom,
should have adopted you.

Sweet'N Low tornado slurry.
The fake sugar falls to the glass floor.

Porcelain

The painted face, delicate, thin, weightless
breaking in my white-knuckled grip. Throwing it
against the wall for emphasis.

This is what we are—
silent rage exploding
into tangibles, collectible
meaning broken, memories building
into tantrum shards that cut flesh,
a genealogy of scars to finger.

Great-grandmother's doll within reach—
the only thing to quiet the yelling.

We change between
mother, daughter, and monster
collecting painted-up pretties to break
into pieces that we throw away.

Everyone Has a Tale

My ancestors can eye up a hen
and predict the lay,
they know coal sparks, mining
darkens lungs to provide,
paraffin preserves the fruits of sun.

My ancestors do not know
botanical nomenclature,
but they can see violet does not suffice
to describe the streak of *johnny jumpups*
that pressed a line
in yesterday's otherwise coral sunset.

They know when to sow seeds,
none having read the Farmer's Almanac,
each has a tale for how to read the wind.
Each has a recipe two pinches different,
but somehow sweeter than mine.

We know full moons are turnstiles,
know when to seal lips, move
along the rimless rip of time.
We know how to gulp silence, go into the dusk
and cry for the return of summer's firefly-quiet night.

Naming

You know,
the tether of longing—
a chasm-crossing strong-arm,
leather stretched   tug tugging.

Our war of tugging—
whole-stomach swallows of loss

reverb and flutter
your heart
a lit wick
flickers with
breath exhaled   to whisper
I miss you—

the feel
of a wax-dipped finger

the peel of the wax flake—
the shape of a petal
no one could name.

Have Mercy

My crooked pinky has two stories:

The time it broke,
I dove to catch a foul ball
in wet grass,
bent it backward
in three-leaf clover
just before the fence.

The time of stitches is known
as my dyke-chest shoved back from the threshold,
not in this house,
door slamming on me
punching through
to sever tendons.
The enemies are known as the devil in me
and mother wielding fists.

My great aunt Flossy said,
God heals if you believe.

Naked but bent fingers all scars.
I dip skillet cornbread in buttermilk,
each mother calls it
their mother's recipe.

Take off

and put back on
my wedding ring,
spread my fingers
into crook-neck dandelions.
Wish.

To reap the roots,
name the mother who loosed the soil,
who held the spade and said,
this is for your own good.

You better call out,
have mercy
with the lord's name

for a reason, *Goddamnit.*

In the Shadows

Grandpa was no simple arc like a scythe
but a spectrum of real moons pale and
mottled, crater-marred phases waning.

Once, Grandma was infrequent
brown eye blinks,
like a young rabbit grazing, ears up,
before being cast in the shadow
of an osprey swooping.

She remembers his guttural grunts,
number three, a slingblade
before the hollering,

her inner ears open petals offer
cutouts, moons, full strawberry and thunder, years
captured in hidden prayer beads
whittled pine, rose quartz, and agate sky.

When we arrived, she said she heard him
say, *I Am sorry*, amidst tears reflecting
hospital fluorescence a-hum-buzzing.

He was scrimshaw, skin like an etched sea.

We let her believe. We stayed for her, softening
our voices in case he could hear us talk
about him in third person. Some paced the halls
as his breath shortened.

On the brink,
we held ours and counted.
We did not unplug the insistence of the monitors.

Disrupting the Literary Narrative

Instruction
Orient the reader, go ahead,
turn it over, take a whiff,
put your tongue to it,
tell them what you taste.
Does its shape conjure something else?
Help them see it, what is it like?
Use a precise color like persimmon or cinnamon.
Tell them how your body feels
and who you miss. Elaborate.
But, use less than four lines to do so.
Pick a loaded symbol.
Add one thing from nature (so you can submit it to
the *Kenyon Review*).
Break the lines, try not to rhyme,
stop when you have three-fourths to one page.

Response
Here, it smells like spit and wood—
the tooth impression on a pencil
tastes like you expect goldenrod to glow
in half-0s. Turn your head sideways,
it's like your cat pressed and held the left
parenthesis key,
then the right in the font Bell MT,
wee weight of a serif—
the ground under your bootprints in snow.
Count the cumulonimbus while

tongue out catching flakes.
Envision you are embodied
as a Douglas Fir
next to the dilapidated garage in your dreams,
the one you want to paint Eggshell.
Inhale and it's grandfather's sawdust,
engine grime, but say
you most remember
the last bite of his
peppered potatoes
fried in bacon grease
not the times you tried
to teach him to read.

How Am I?

I almost want to thank Mother's cancer.
Hope stripped with each change
of sheets, now just globules of mercury
rolling on the tile floor,
stopping in cracks—
the way you feel when
you've removed roller skates,
replaced shoes,
swung a lead bat
before an aluminum.
The sudden lightness propels you
into a way off balance.

Envoy

He drives her home like always, after
the thin dripping tubes are disconnected,
in the giant vehicle she picked out.
He'd prefer a pickup,
a motorcycle, the freedom
from monthly payments.

She tires easily, is losing some of her fight.
It isn't shrinking like they'd expected
but she doesn't say so,
says they are doing radiation instead of surgery.
She speaks of the doctor's admiration—
says she's a survivor.

It's early afternoon, the sun beats the car
into a drowsy naplike breath,
a kind of pulse coursing veins—
the road home.
He drives but isn't,
instead he's thinking
of the arrangements,
how he'll sell the house, what he'll buy.
He's imagining old buddies from the fire station
coming with awkward embraces
expressing their pat condolences,
leaving with harder pats on the back,
pats that push him into the life
he's wanted to live for so long.

Desperation

We tell ourselves we don't know any better.

Were all on this life-ride like a rickshaw
on cobblestone, driver without a license.

Curb to curb, the rage of dependence
will never be digested, our stomachs always
waiting for something other than hunger
for what isn't.

My need for a mother's love,
the same desperation as galloping
when called no matter it's midnight,
the same as my long-distance partner and I
driving I-5 ten hours every ten days.

A fix ripples through the body, a slow tremble.
Don't you swallow and tell yourself that it is need?

Just a tongue drop of nectar to keep flitting,
to hover awkwardly in a blur, a photograph cannot
capture the copper iridescence of
the ultimately disappointing wingspan.

We are always clamoring, aggregating,
attaching, hoping we aren't really alone
striving toward impossible satiation.

Mercy

If you ask me in person, I'll say
I'm glad my mother is dead.
But when I dream, I long for her grimace.
I want her mouth
        open tonsil-big shouting—
a window in the fuddle of grief.
But, I want her
to shout through the broken
glass fist-shattered by my 15-year-old
dyke-not-her-daughter severed tendons.
I want her
to shout through her family's
        Baptist *Yor-goin-to-hell* condemnations
To shout through her head-
shaken-side-to-side *NO*.
I want to hear
spittle, slobber flying as fists
I want her pounding glass
with urgency
like the dream is filling with water,
I want her
desperate even if just to save herself.
I really want to know,
can you hear
the sound of a daughter's hands
on her mother's throat?
Can you hear

    the mother say *You are My baby, always will be*
Or do you hear
    her say *No daughter of mine…*
Do you leave it unexamined?
Can you see us now?
Without pry or pound, I need things from her mouth.
But, no one can hear *I'm sorry*
    before our mouths fill with water
    and become just warble and bubbles.

The Language Of Arms

Opening, closing around bodies,
ours more downed branches
gathered by a bystander,
dangled across a chasm we all pruned

to disguise our last portrait
of half-smile embraces
the scrutiny of
uncle-cousin-aunt-eyes snapshotting

the guilty dropping of our arms
before mother's final let go,
we blinked our own shudder/shuttering
that death-winter, Dad raked our modesty
and we turned from the windows not to see,
not to be seen covering
our most private parts stripped.

Grenade

Cervical cancer has no grace, makes no apologies.
Mother had never called for my help before.

*Help me, there's a thing coming out of me
"down there."*

She needed me to see the clot—
a pomegranate, a rotten baby.

Just get it out of me.

She'd been hemorrhaging
the family's whole visit.
Trembling, knowing
I could be what killed her,
ended all of this.
Knowing, if I were to touch her there,
a swarm of bees would kick up off
bite-ridden fruit
in her father's backyard.

Just get it out of me.

I tried, twisted
right, left
ripping a bit,
my hand cradling
the warmth, the weight.

I could not hold. Fix it, fix anything.
I called Dad. He called hospice.
I rattled out two Vicodin, Lorazepam—
her razzle dazzles—
a blue and white swallow to the sky.

I can't take this many.

Her blood crusting my fingernails,
she worried I'd given her too many pills.

Now, I nurse the ghosts
with my own liftings—

knowing weeks shortened to days
in my adopted hands.

Today, I pluck seeds and savor
the taste of stain.

I Drink

Mother'd been dying for a year.
I only picked up half the calls, answered them all
by turning to pour. I drank.

I cupped a cigarette in the rain, smoked.
Lifted a bottle after each exhale. I drank.

I last kissed her cheek too close to her neck,
remembered choking.

While they quieted the cry out
to moans with morphine, I drank.

A brown spider big as my palm on the eave
not yet inside but too close preying.
I watched him rest, waiting in his web.

I looked for days to the ladybugs for humanity,
watched them crawling over their dead
amassing in the lamp of my living room.
Didn't see a point clearing them
until the season changed. I drank.

Too Late

The illusion of what she is, what
he is, what I am
recedes. Once there's a hospital bed, everything
begins to fall away.

I start to hear echoes

Hold your shoulders back,
Did you wash your hands,
and then,
It's time to prepare for me not to be here.

The call came late.
Your mother passed away
two   hours   ago.

I searched crawl spaces in my mind,
anything that signaled her passing.

A throng of gentle wings
like waves lapping,
a nausea, the rising of
a hundred swallows out of ash
gripping me at the back of my neck.

Secrets slated for burial
crawling in my throat.
So much remains unsaid:

Hold your shoulders back.
Wash your hands.

Epitaph

Two weeks left of dying. I overheard her
whispering to the cousins,
Lisa might keep me from going to heaven.

Eyes now so sunken from morphine, half open,
her pupils are little lichen covered headstones.

I didn't read *Loving Mother of Lisa Renee*,
I saw sky,
cloudwork reconfiguring death as
cumulus beasts of parent and child, a sun
glaring as an interrogation bulb, a lawn of
tiny faceless children, their murmur
either hope or help. My mind
humming, fumbling to find
an answer approximating tenderness. Dad tracing
his fingers across her
face, illuminating grave memory.

I imagine he tired of taking
out the trash, of the bloody
chuck pads, of asking
my cousin to buy more sheets, of
sleepless nights listening
to her labored breath,
of the phone, of updating,
of leaving me voicemails,
of having family, friends in and out
all hours, instead he tells me,

you know she loved you the best that she could.

This bridge is not constructed well for the crossing.

You are freed to float
for days. Waiting for the rasp
to release into light.

Now, we know when
there are white candles burning
next to white candles in
churches, at ceremonies—
silent cries of light, burning
the unanswered leave.

Dad tells me he remembers
a weak smile he hopes
was for him, but can accept
it was for her Maker.

I am the lesbian flying
in late. I arrive in Vera Wang,
platinum cross,
2 inch heels,
MAC makeup,
and silence in absence of a ring
on my left hand.

Standing next to her casket looking out on
the congregation, all eyes full,
offering to acknowledge

a life I couldn't,

even in drag.

Death and life both crave
clarity, light. Obituary
and poetry spark and carry
until we run out
of wax and wick.

Dust

Count the years of trying in
wooden Mother's Day angels.

One with a lantern.
One with a book.
One with a butterfly.

Wishes for approval, apology—
now dust from these things
caught in the vents.

If only,
all I gave her was light to read and fly.

Mother and I wielded words like shovels.
Digging.
Always digging.

I've been trying to forget the way
her hands looked
in the casket—

not quite together, not
touching each other, but
magnetized by her own polarity—

I like to think the gap is regret.

Fists Are the Size of Hearts

I see you laid out on cold steel,
your back propped with a body block,
arms and neck stretched back
pushing your chest upward, saying *take me.*

I cut deep,
down to your pubic bone,
lay my hand flat and try to take back
childhood bruising to cleanse, to free you—
exposing the white keys of your ribs, I practice
my concert piece, practice,
practice again, trying to make perfect, but
your dead weight flattens the song, your
complete lack of participation
disheartens me.

I keep thinking your lips will
peel open like super glued fingers separated
to scream, *no one will ever love you.*
The knife gleaming reflection,
I see myself scary
as I did after we choked each other.

I cut skin, rip
open your chest, two fists pulled apart quick
remind me of a belt snapping.
Cutting through to
carefully scalpel tissue with a surgical blade

like the one I stole to slit at my numbness.

I want to replace your heart with
a clock, a pacemaker different than your father's,
one I set, to free you, me of all those times—
but only a bit with each second's tick. So, by the time
we meet again, we can both forgive.

Bessie

In dreams, Mother's hands reach from the coffin
toward me, try to
pull me back into
her wind's tongue-lash, last words, her name:
BESS, Bessie, extra esses, whistle-screech,
sky flipped, rumble, strike, storm—
purple, gray, a lifted skirt, a cloud, no slip
whip-weaves burial dirt, cigarette ash,
gravestone rubble dust and autumn's turnt leaves—

there's so much white:
candles, coffin lining, calla lilies—
funeral flickers flash snapshots stitched,
our uneven seams sewn, sealed with swigs,
blood-stained sheets snapping
like flags for each season,
so much rubbish to clear, it is the Midwest.
I am gulping mouth swallows,
glass bottles, kissing cold, coffin handles,
a platinum cross,
ghost hands,
I hold tight.

Catharsis

Each photo lighter-lit and set to embers.
Snapped apertures, struck faces, strained.
Cakes for ages, Christmas tree poses,

the big gift held up like grandpa's big bass.

The catch—
a collapse like her casket
calla lilies, one slow week of wilting,
the finality of *nothing we can do* cancer—

a hot burn, a quick-tempered fuse
quietly releasing ultramarine, cyan, family history—
little hisses caving.

Each flavescent, saffron-tipped
birthday candle waiting
for its *never tell* wish—
take time, but remember
the quick, amnesiac ease of flames.

Try to name the colors in fire
like there's a spell:
carmine, cinnabar,
sienna, rust.
Repeat:
Mother, I raze to salvage you.

Craning to the stars, watch

ashes bluster, blow ancestral white
kisses to the wind.
Wait agape—
a bundled child catching her first flakes.

Fishing

In a dream, my dead mother came to me
as a big ass, big mouth bass.
Yes, human size,
ability to speak
though slobbery.
I pulled up to a lake
in a red Honda CRV,
and she hopped
from the water's edge to the car.
Finned open the door,
slosh-hopped into my backseat
exasperated, told me I was late.
I can't remember anything else.

Don't forget Grandpa loved to fish.
Mother's name was Bess.
The unconscious conflates.
Remember that Billy the Bass fad?

Grief wishes it was as easy as mounting
your dead on a plaque
to play any phrase from their mouth over
and again.

The Logic of Dreams—Freudian, Predictable

Sometimes Mother comes to me disguised

as geraniums, red buds—
    loose fists of painted nails
a slight swaying in terracotta
    stinky sweet, she comes as rusty shears
on the wrought iron table—
    fishnet shadows on concrete.
This dream has allure—
    the trappings of a first date,
atomic red, touchable texture, sharp, perfumed,
    leaning into an awkward dance.

Bring its mordacity to my mouth,
    let's rip grief's bandaid off,
quick like her doctor delivering the news.

Comfort

Still writing the same affected-by-
her-death poems. But,
grief isn't fire, can't be
squelched by tears, isn't fooled
by bourbon's smoky sadism.
Her echo is no longer a wind-whipped
trees-transferred-from-one-town-to-another disaster.

I should shut up.
I am no longer, every day,
thinking of her rough hands in the casket—
knowing the cruel never make peace.
No longer motherless, I now know comfort
in arms of consistency, softness
in blue eyes.

What I want now is fried chicken,
mashed potatoes,
extra gravy,
and good drugs.

Smile For Me, Honey

I'm tired of being asked if I'm okay.
So you know, it's like this when I say, yes, fine:

You best hold tight to your dears,
my brain's a wrigglin' like
a mass of feral cats—
a felted fur caul, tiny claws
out for breath and blood not their own.

I'm adopted. To me, it's all just
breath and innards, inner workings, working
their way out, some better than others.
Mother, Mothers, sister, sisters?—

I can't help but think of Medusa, working out
her head, someone saying, smile for me honey,
trying to bag her, all hisses and nips, an
angry tangle, scales sloughing,
and pity the fool that unpacks that bag.

I am a bitch, I know
some have a pulse that will warm you,
even slink veins to suck out the slag,
can examine close,
shatter, gnaw, and truly see you
through your mean. But, remember,
Hazel is just a nice way to say
eyes change with rage;
and it's still my reflection in those
train-flattened-

penny-pupils.

I should smile more. It's not that bad.

So Many Deaths This Year

We spoon
mashed potatoes
off paper poinsettia plates—

ashes and burial earth
in our all-quiet mouths.

Homosexuals More Likely to Develop Bipolar Disorder

ABSTRACT: *This study strongly suggests that rates of bipolar disorder are higher among homosexual females compared to general population samples. The study seeks to provide imagery in the brain of a homosexual female in a state of mania. There are confounding variables in this study: Subject is an adoptee and was rejected by her adopted mother for her sexual proclivities and hallucinations, she was believed to be "of the devil" before, during, and after diagnosis.*

INTRODUCTION: Baptists don't believe in visage or voice, unless divine—like capital "H," *He has risen*. Even dead voices, incant, and call for you. Forget the moment in the bathtub before metal caught the glint. Kev said, *maybe mercy means it's possible to love things you hate.*

METHODS: Your greatest power comes from your deepest wound.

Figure 1:

Light a blue candle, stare
at the flame long enough to
outshine the stars

tiny hands clasping,
glass jars, lids forked to let air flow

imagine blood like comets sluicing
veins at 240 beats,
light-full organs glowing,
dimmer switch to the max.

let's go back to the time before
I knew
stone, gravel can strengthen,

not just scrape-break skin

let's go back to the time before

the voltage of lightning

in the dark
think—fireflies—
sexual pyrotechnics
wink a double flash,

still, believe in the luminary

let's go back to the time before I knew
some(one)thing that gives
stability

let's go back to the time before
the fall and break
and hold

times, I couldn't stabilize my current

blood gave me

the sky—a bruised shelf cloud.

RESULTS: Manic body bioluminescent, raising arms, preparing to take flight. A sparrow or a swift (I get confused) but a euphemism told me the silence between soaring and landing is spirit. But every movement makes a sound. Compose a sermon, a spell, stretch a rubber band to hold this like this together, a deep vibrato resounds when isolated and plucked, listen to the chords, louder, louder, imagine a piano, pedal pushed or an organ's pipe dream. I'm interested in the bass of a story but the lyrics fly away with the chorus. Surround me like that house where she died. She keeps coming in echos: *you are lucky you were born, you are lucky you were, you are lucky you.*

CONCLUSION:
Tension is always deciding its breaking point. There is always a before.

Shaping Desire

It's not just the "O" of
glossed lips on the mirror—
all glass reflects her.

It's not just electric,
it's neon. Red-pink, blue bruises—
an open sign.

She's not just the blinding sun—
she is when you blink
to stare again.

It's not just the feel
of a pop-popping drum—
it's that feel of the uh-uhing bass.

It's not just the throb—
it's a tapping—a thimble
on another Mother's thumb thrumming—
it's the smell of tin,
it's hollowing—
an open can
tasting knife-sharp,
ratcheting breath—

it's you holding the lid a-dangle
in your trembling fingers,
and knowing my need is—
a final tear to let go.

Barometer

I know *you* are not her.
But what is your measure
for a bad day.

You've never seen a roof ripped off
of a barn, sucked up in a vortex,
a thousand black shingles
like a whirlwind of ravens
conjured in your name,
all the expletives preceding.

During the years of lightning, in seasons,
she twisted through my countryside with her
slipshod picking up of precious things,
dropped them all thoughtless, slapdash
into the lives of others.

With you, I don't have to assess the aftermath,
pile up the splintered boards
burst from behind shutters, or sweep up broken glass.

I pray we are all cumulus clouds and calm breezes—
All I want is the amnesia of trees this spring.

Some Dance to Remember, Some Dance to Forget

Birthmom tells me the last song on her car radio
before she went in to give birth to me.

April 24, 1978
sounds like the Eagles,
smells like Salem Lights,
looks like a water-broke waddle

Up ahead in the distance, I saw a shimmering light.
I want to know was the swift removal of me
pre-planned?

Relax said the night man, we are programmed to receive.
Was there some white-suited nurse, pursed lip of
judgment, poised to swoop me off after the snip?

My head grew heavy and my sight grew dim.
Did the nurse ask you then,
out of epidurals, eyes opening, closing. One last push

There were voices down the corridor...
Did you close your eyes
while your mother spoke for you?

I had to find the passage back to the place I was before
Mom, tell me,
you didn't say, *no,*
I don't want to hold her.

Naming

A name is a fingerprint,
a cartography.
The whorls an identity given
before all the scars—

Birthmom says,
I named you Jessica.
Always shortened it, used to whisper,
Jessie, I love you.

To finally be told what my name is.
To read that it means gift.

To try it on for fit,
hem it to JS or Jess.
But, catch myself turning in the Bart or
bar when someone calls Jessie.

I have an origin.

Trace me back.

Count the rings,
press tips for story,
roll the ink,
I'll spin Scrimager truths
line for line.

A name is a heartbeat—
the repetition, thump thu thump—
each letter's stroke
crafts a signature, my mom gave me her initials, JS,
curves to hold me.

When you say Jessie,
I can hear the wisp
of my forehead curl
swept back for a mother's kiss.

Reflection at 45

My therapist said, *write a poem about your adopted dad.*

It's the same old story: he slammed doors, rattled
glass, used fists, and left.
I haven't told you, he was my role model and coach,
a lesser monster than mother.

I've told you my mother said,
You dyke, you're no daughter of mine,
as she slammed that door, and I threw my
right fist through a pane of glass.
I haven't described pulling glass
from my pointer finger,

the outpouring blood spray spatter like a Rorschach
on the patio concrete. Or the Wendy's Biggie cup
Mother threw at me to bleed into.

I waited 1, 2, 3 hours
for Dad to come home
and take me to the hospital.

I haven't told you Dad didn't apologize,
didn't fight for me,
but always made me say, I'm sorry to her.

I haven't told you that I learned from him
anger is an emotion that swells

like a snake with each large swallow.

I haven't told you I harbor resentment
at absence and disregard,
especially the damn near impossible gift of,
I'm proud of you, kid.

I haven't told you I hold it in my body,
hold it in my sewn tight tendon fingers that don't bend,
hold it in my shoulder ache as inflammation

strangles a nerve, the stars it shoots
remind me of the snap of my shoulder—
the all star tournament I pitched to win for him,

fingers lined on stitching, counting 1, 2, 3,
the windmill windup to deliver
the last strike, a no-hitter.

Like the illegal bottle rockets he bought for me,
nights we'd count together before the sky
erupted—flash and boom,
the nights she'd count his fists as grenades— *1,2,3...*

Count the bruises, wait the days
until they'd yellow out, when
Maybelline could help.

My blood is still, 10, 20, 30 years later,

open to interpretation

underfoot another owner's story of privacy.

I hope they got a new back door,
a different threshold.

acknowledgements

First, Mom, Julie Scrimager Kern, thank you for the artistic DNA, the opportunity to create, and the love that exists beyond this earthly plane. To Bess G, for the complicated family dynamics, your character, stories, pain, and all the times you meant well. Phil G, thank you for the countless sacrifices and hours you worked to provide for me and for teaching me that words have power.

To my wife, Krista, thanks for your unwavering support, for being a first reader, for attending countless poetry readings, and for uplifting my work and encouraging me always. Your unconditional love, patience, fishnets, and fried chicken sustained me through the highs and lows of this creative process.

A sincerely heartfelt thank you to all my friends who showed up hard with encouragement, workshops, prompts, 420 writing sessions, CLEAVEs, advice, laughter, and a generous ear when I often needed to chat it out. Your support helped me birth this book baby. Special shout out to Will G and my poetry fam, Cleavage Collective.

I extend my upmost appreciation to Kevin, my best associative thought partner, my editor, and my publisher. Your talent, time, friendship, and dedication to the craft encourage and motivate me to push myself creatively. Thank you for believing in my work and bringing it to a wider audience.

To my mentors and advisors, your guidance and wisdom have been instrumental in shaping this book. Shout out to Pacific University, Lambda Literary, and Tin House faculty and students. Your insights and constructive feedback have been instrumental through the creative process.

To my best editor, Snacks, thank you for all of the times you stepped on my keyboard or laid on top of my poems to let me know they weren't finished yet, and thank you for your patience on the bathroom rug while I read poetry to you from the tub.

Much gratitude to the editors and curators of these publications and spaces where some of these poems were first housed in different forms: "Mercy" & "Fists are the Size of Hearts" in *sPARKLE & bLINK*, "Catharsis" in *Syzygy*, "Have Mercy" in *Sad Girl Diaries*, and premiering the "Barometer" video poem at Streetlight Guild's Rhapsody & Refrain: 30 Columbus Poets.

Finally, thank you to the readers who embark on this journey with me. Your engagement and appreciation make the countless hours of writing worthwhile. I hope this book challenges the adoption narrative, punches you in the gut, jerks tears, and elicits gasps, laughter, and smiles. Thank you! Thank you! Thank you!

Sincerely,
JSG

education guide

not my daughter is a mesmerizing collection of 44 poems that are part confessional, part documentary, part analytical lyric exploration of the adoption system, part southern baptist parentage and queer identity narrative, part psychedelic sensual love story of the self and others, part meditation on loss and processing of grief with a complicated relationship, part, part, part. As you will find throughout, "this is my body, / broken for you," it contains multitudes.

This book is primarily through the lens of what it means to be a daughter, and we get to explore this expanse with that framework and a wonderful guide.

Jessie is a poetic auteur of technical brilliance, singular personality, and deep interior meaning who immerses the reader in a universe through the use of her textured world which, even though it's only a slice, feels whole.

When she "last kissed her [mother's] cheek too close to her neck, / remembered choking," we're present. When we're shown "calla lilies, one slow week of wilting," we experience the feeling of "the finality of nothing we can do cancer." When she asks, "Do you leave it unexamined?" We consider how being "in the fuddle of grief" shapes the present and our future reflections.

When we read these luminous, dynamic poems filled with beauty and grief and desire, we learn ways to examine ourselves, our relationships, and others through new perspectives. And we are able to glean many truths, such as how "Death and life both crave / clarity, light" or how "We are always clamoring, aggregating, / attaching, hoping we aren't really alone / striving toward impossible satiation."

This collection of poems shows the influence of its tradition: the tight narratives of Dorianne Laux, the disruption and complications of narratives like Natalie Diaz or Victoria Chang, the relentlessly beautiful lyrics of Diane Seuss, the rhythm-obsession of Sylvia Plath but with the natural pockets of Patricia Smith along with the emotional depth and care of subject matter as Ellen Bass, and a way of engaging with the world through eyes of wonder as Tomas Tranströmer or Ross Gay.

discussion guide

One of the masterful techniques we can learn from Jessie Scrimager Galloway's poetry in this collection is how she is able to ground us in three-dimensional worlds across moments in scenes.

She does it in several ways: sensory use of space, light, texture, and more. **What did you notice?** For now, let's focus on how she uses *word blending*. Many are highlighted by hyphen use, but not all are. She elevates these compounded phrases beyond portmanteau to create a lexicon of blended dimensions which embody what's happening for the reader.

Notice, not just the hyphenated words, but the phrases around them. **How does she orient the reader in a place?** Here are a few of the word blends:

- *her wind's tongue-lash*
- *photo lighter-lit*
- *half-smile embraces*
- *uncle-cousin-aunt-eyes snapshotting*
- *slosh-hopped into my backseat*

From the examples above, Jessie writes how wind comes from a tongue "lashing," giving dimension to the idiom and highlighting the physical aspects. She writes that the photo is set on fire, specifically with a lighter in hand. She tells us that there are embraces, but shows us that they are with half-smiles which also gives a depth and texture to how that embrace might be. She shows us close-ups of the eyes as well as a whole room full of family taking pictures of one another simultaneously.

How can you incorporate word blending in your writing?

writing prompt

1. Write a poem that takes place during an argument with one person who attempts to leave the room. *Make sure you don't simply write dialogue but also give sensory details about the space, objects, and has an interior metaphor-making like Jessie's work.*
2. Take that poem (or any of your poems) and underline moments that you feel are most important, give an image, convey an action, or use any of the senses. Look for moments to conjoin multiple words to give another dimension to your phrasing which might give texture to the feelings around what's happening instead of writing those feelings directly.

video poem

scan above or visit:

https://bit.ly/barometer-video

music playlist

scan above or visit:

https://bit.ly/not-my-daughter-music

Photo credit: Reina Vazquez

Jessie Scrimager Galloway is an adopted, queer poet with mommy issues. She is a graduate of Pacific University's MFA program and author of the chapbook, *Liminal: A Life of Cleavage* (Lost Horse Press). She loves her wife's fried chicken and conversations with her best editor: Snacks, a wily, polydactyl, orange cat.